THE

GRACE
BASED

LIFE

Dion —
Enjoy & Be Blessed
Tom Goetz

THE

GRACE
BASED

LIFE

TOM GOETZ

Pleasant Word (a division of WinePress Publishing, PO Box 428, Enumclaw, WA 98022) functions only as book publisher. As such, the ultimate design, content, editorial accuracy, and views expressed or implied in this work are those of the author.

ISBN 13: 978-1-4141-1313-5
ISBN 10: 1-4141-1313-7
Library of Congress Catalog Card Number: 2010901246

CONTENTS

INTRODUCTION

I F YOU HAVE felt discouraged, disillusioned, or defeated because your efforts to live the Christian life have ended mostly in frustration and failure, this book is for you.

I hope that by reading it you will be able to quit trying so hard and will take the first step in letting God do for you what you are trying to do for yourself. In short, I want to introduce you to the grace-based life, the life God had in mind for you when He created you.

God never intended for you to live on the basis of your own strength and resources. From the very beginning, He planned to do for you those things you are unable to do for yourself and to provide for you those things you are unable to provide for yourself. That's the essence of the grace-based life—living in the authenticity of God's provision rather than in the counterfeit substitutes of our own creation.

Legitimate human needs fill every life, and we spend much of life attempting to get those needs met. But when God created us, He also created the means to meet our needs. For example, everyone needs love, and God planned to meet that requirement through our parents and other significant people in our lives. Sometimes it doesn't work the way He intended, and a vacuum develops in our lives. If God's authentic provision of Himself and other believers does not then fill the void, counterfeits or substitutes will almost certainly fill it, which leaves us with another problem: counterfeits and substitutes simply don't satisfy. So we are left with at least part of our need still unmet. When people go from one unsatisfying relationship to another, for example, they are simply trying to fill the emotional vacuum that still exists from the last unsatisfying relationship. Many people attempt to build their entire lives on a foundation of counterfeit and substitute provisions, until at some point something happens that causes their whole life to come crashing down.

In the same way, many Christians attempt to build their spiritual lives on counterfeit and substitute provisions by building on a foundation of self-effort rather than on a foundation of grace. If you are one of them, you will eventually become exhausted, begin to lose hope, and probably reach the conclusion that you cannot achieve the results you desire. Before you reach this point, let me encourage you to read this little book and discover the possibilities of a grace-based life. God doesn't want your efforts to end in frustration and failure. I don't want that for you, and I know you don't want it either.

When God entered your life, He began the process of replacing the substitutes and counterfeits in your life with His authentic provision. As you cooperate with Him, you will progressively begin to live the life God designed for you—built on a foundation that consists of the power of His promises and the promise of His power. Living the grace-based life is about building on God's authentic provision rather than on a foundation of counterfeits and substitutes. It's about moving past the frustration and failure of self-effort into the freedom and power of allowing God to provide what you can't provide for yourself as you live out God's design for your life.

When God created you, He planned for you to enjoy an abundant life under His care. Have you settled for a life of counterfeits and substitutes, or are you depending on God to fill your every need? To find out, let's examine what it means to live a grace-based life.

CHAPTER 1

THE LOOK OF
THE GRACE-BASED LIFE

THE ESSENCE OF the grace-based life is found in two transformational spiritual dynamics: the power of promise and the promise of power. We need both of these to live life as God designed it.

To live with the *power of promise* means to live with the strength and perseverance that come from hope and vision. It means living in the realm of possibilities, daring to believe in destiny and potential. This kind of life results from doing things God's way and finding solutions to the challenges of life that produce lasting results and give hope and strength for the long haul.

The power of promise whispers this life-shaping secret to your soul: your life is more than the sum of your actions and struggles, for you are a person with a God-designed future. You are a significant member of His family and part of His plan for creation. The power of promise energizes you and transforms you into the essence of what it means to be "a new creation in Christ" (2 Cor. 5:17), but you need more than this to live the grace-based life.

While the power of promise represents the possibilities of life, it is the *promise of power* that transforms those possibilities into reality. Promise without power will produce frustration, but promise with power is God's design for life. It's God saying, "I have a destiny for you, and I will use my unlimited power to see that your destiny becomes your reality. I will do for you what you can't do for yourself so you can live life as I designed it." That's grace at work.

Grace is that supernatural touch from God that enables us to become what we could never become without His help. Grace is God's attitude toward us turned into action for our benefit. Since He is *for* us, He helps us do what we are unable to do through our own strength and efforts.

The foundation of the grace-based life is the power of promise and the promise of power. Before you begin to build on that foundation, however, you need a vision of what you are building. In other words, you need to know the look of the grace-based life.

The Grace-Based Life Is Free of Counterfeit Miracles or Provisions

Our lives are shaped by a combination of predominant influences that determine the kind of life we will experience. Some are shaped by the influence of their relationship with Jesus Christ and the provisions of God in every area of life, while others are shaped by the combined influence of the "four Ss"—Satan, sin, society, and self—and what they provide. Can you identify which has the most influence in your life? Since each of these influences produces very different results, you need to be able to recognize which is predominant in your life.

In reality the four Ss are nothing more than four false gods that we turn to with the mistaken idea that these gods can provide everything we need to live a meaningful, significant, and satisfying life. Nothing could be further from the truth. Whatever we worship will ultimately shape our lives, and whatever we grant godlike power we will worship. Giving godlike power to a false or counterfeit god results in a life filled with counterfeit miracles and provisions, which in turn are indicators of a life being shaped by the influence of the four Ss.

For example, consider technology and wealth, two areas of life to which many people in our culture have given godlike power. More and more people are placing their hope and faith in technology and wealth with the idea that these will provide what they need to live a fulfilled life. Technology and wealth are vital areas of modern life, but each has a downside.

It's one thing for nonbelievers to turn to these false gods, but when the people of God do the same thing, we force God's hand. He has told His people we are not to have any other gods before Him. Probably nothing illustrates my point more than the deceptive thinking of those who turn to the lottery gods in America, hoping that somehow this idolatrous relationship will provide everything they need.

Believers who turn to the false gods of the lottery for provision are in reality attempting to bypass the laws of creation set in place by the Creator from the beginning. One of the laws of creation is the law of the harvest—sowing and reaping—and as we sow our financial seed in accordance with this spiritual law, we will receive a harvest in due season. However, many of God's people plant some of their financial seed in accordance with the law of chance, hoping the lottery god will reward their worship with a great harvest. They fail to understand that if they win, they have received a counterfeit provision from a false god, and at the same time have opened the door to real spiritual consequences. Playing the lottery is an attempt to create our own miracle with the help of a false god, and that is not a wise thing to do.

So if you don't mind counterfeit miracles in your life, and if you don't mind putting yourself in a position where God has to remove them to show you that you have indeed been experiencing counterfeit provisions, and if you don't mind giving your worship to a false god that will eventually be challenged and destroyed by the one true God, and if you don't mind risking the displeasure of the God who will have no other gods before Him, and if you don't mind bowing down at the altar of the lottery gods—then by all means play the lottery. But understand this: it is not an innocent game. Worshipping false gods does have spiritual consequences.

The Grace-Based Life Is Filled with Spiritual Strength and Energy

Freedom from counterfeit miracles and provision is only one of the benefits of living a grace-based life. Living life the way God designed it also means we will develop the strength and stamina necessary to finish in victory.

People whose lives are built on a foundation of promise and power will always have enough spiritual strength to finish their race. This is not the case with a life under the influence of the four Ss. When Satan, sin, society, and self are the primary influences in a life, we soon find ourselves relying on personal strength and human wisdom to manage life's challenges, which always results in spiritual fatigue and exhaustion. There is a reason this happens.

The Bible tells us there is a way that seems right to people but leads to death. (Prov. 14:12) All of the ways that can seem right to us have two things in common: they promise quick answers and results, and they promise easy answers and results. As members of the microwave generation, that's what we are looking for, quick and easy. We don't want to wait for anything. We certainly don't want anything to be difficult; we don't want to struggle. If something involves sacrifice, we aren't interested.

If we want to live life the way God designed it, we have to do things God's way, and His ways are not like our ways" (Prov. 14:12). His ways also have two things in common: He is never in a hurry, and his way is almost always the more difficult option.

Take marriage, for instance. God's plan calls for a man and a woman to enter into a covenant with each other, and until they do, they are not to enter into a sexual relationship. When the struggles and challenges of marriage come, this covenant will hold them together. Man's way focuses on the quick-and-easy approach to marriage. People who follow this way ignore the element of covenant and opt for "living together," not understanding the eventual consequences of this decision. Since living together is quick and easy, splitting up when the challenges come is also quick and easy. The relationship never has a chance to become what God intended and designed it to be.

In marriage the husband and wife become one, but that transformation doesn't happen quickly, easily, or cheaply. For a man and woman to become one as God intended takes time. The qualities needed result from choices each makes that might require considerable struggle and change. First, of course, they must choose to stay together through the process of transformation.

Now here is the irony of turning to quick and easy solutions for our problems: human thinking says that the struggle and difficulty of doing things God's way will wear us out—it's too hard and we won't survive the process—but in reality the opposite is true. The struggles and challenges that often accompany God's ways make us stronger and transform us into people of endurance. Doing something God's way when our way would be quicker and easier builds character and produces long-term strength. God's way trains us, gets us into shape, and gives us the ability to finish the race.

The irony is that the quick-and-easy approach doesn't build anything in us for the extra mile. We discover that in trying to protect ourselves, we have in fact weakened ourselves, so that when the struggles and challenges continue, we are left standing in our own inadequate strength and wisdom. We don't have the extra measure of strength we would have gained from doing things God's way, and we are left in a place of emotional and spiritual fatigue. The irony is that quick and easy produces overload and exhaustion! Quick and easy is the way of the false gods of our culture.

If you want to remain strong to the end, choose God's way to handle the challenges and issues of life. Even though it is almost always the more difficult way, it is also the only way to develop the strength and stamina needed to finish the journey well and ensure success in the challenging arena of human relationships.

THE GRACE-BASED LIFE ENJOYS SECURE RELATIONSHIPS

Another part of the promise and power of the grace-based life is the security found in the relationships that develop because they contain a built-in covenant factor.

When we approach relationships with the quick-and-easy, no-struggle method, we don't develop relationships strong enough to stand in the face of challenges. Quick and easy produces tremendous insecurity, and insecurity prevents a relationship from becoming the kind of personal bond most people strongly desire. Insecure people feel the need to protect themselves and to hold back. When one or both partners hold back, they are not able to become one the way God intended. Apply this to the number of people living together without the security of a covenant-based marriage and it becomes easy to understand why we are becoming a generation of dysfunctional marriages and families.

For a relationship to prosper, whether a marriage or a friendship, it must have an environment of security—without fear of rejection—in which to grow. If you take security out of marriage, one of the partners will become a performer, acting out a role and never feeling free to develop and grow as an individual. A fragile, shallow marriage is the result, which is unsatisfying to both partners, and the marriage becomes a house of cards that can tumble down at any moment. Because the partners don't want to bring their house of cards tumbling down, they will withdraw and hold back even more. In the end they are left with a marriage that has been shaped through the influence of the four Ss instead of God's perfect plan.

A Grace-Based Alternative

If you don't want to live life with counterfeit miracles and provisions, and if you don't want to go through life with no security in your relationships because they have no covenant factor, the alternative is the grace-based life, lived through the influence of a relationship with Jesus Christ and shaped by the power of promise and the promise of power.

If you're ready to embrace a life characterized by these two transformational spiritual truths, then let's get started by examining the foundation on which you are building your life.

CHAPTER 2

EXAMINING YOUR SPIRITUAL FOUNDATION

IN OUR DESIRE to become the people God has called us to be, we are often tempted to skip over some of the very issues and processes that make transformation possible. For example, we often move from one stage of the building process to the next before we are ready and before God has given us permission to do so. The little two-word saying, "God permitting," represents an absolutely essential element of becoming the person God calls us to be.

In any type of building project, one of the first requirements is to get a permit to build. Once the builders have completed the first stage of the project, they must notify the building inspector, who comes and inspects what they have built to determine if it's up to code. If the building project meets acceptable standards, the inspector checks off the permit and allows the builders to proceed to the next stage of the project. If the inspector doesn't check off the permit, the builders must go back and fix whatever is wrong before proceeding.

Hebrews 6:1–3 talks about allowing God to inspect what we are building, beginning with our foundation. In this passage God is the building inspector and our spiritual life is the building being constructed. The first two verses identify six spiritual concepts that need to be part of the foundation on which we are building. God examines the foundation to see if those six foundational concepts are in place and producing what He designed them to produce in our life. If the foundation does not pass inspection, we will need to repair it before we try to construct the rest of the building. In many ways the foundation is the most important part of the building process.

Perhaps the most important reason for letting God inspect the foundation of our life is to be sure it will support what God wants to build on it. Many believers have constructed lives that appear to be well grounded, but upon close inspection we discover that their foundation is unable to support the life God had in mind for them. What a great tragedy it would be to one day stand before God only to discover that we missed the life He wanted to give us simply because we didn't have the foundation to support it! That's why it's so important to let God examine the foundation of our life. We want to be sure it will support what he wants to do for us, to us, and through us.

Will Our Foundation Survive the Storms That Come Against It?

We want to be sure that the foundation we are building has the strength to stand the tests it will face in life.

Matthew 7:24–27 deals with the issue of testing. In this short parable, Jesus talked about two men who each built a house as an illustration of how they were building their lives. The only apparent difference between the two was the foundation on which they each built—one on a foundation of sand and the other on a foundation of rock. Everything appeared to be OK with both houses until a storm approached. When the elements of the storm began to pound these two houses, the one built on sand collapsed but the one built on rock survived the storm.

We live in a generation impressed with appearances, a generation that doesn't like to wait, and so we find people who have learned to build lives that looks spiritual by using the right words and doing the right things—and doing so quickly. But if this is you, when you've encountered a powerful life storm, you discovered that your foundation lacked the strength to survive, and the building that looked so good, so spiritual, and so strong came tumbling down.

Whatever the form of a life storm, it will reveal the strength of a life's foundation. Sometimes the storm comes in the form of temptations we are not prepared to handle, sometimes in the form of pressure or persecution. Often the storm comes when we discover that God wants to change us or the way we live. A storm may come even in the form of God's blessings. Often I've seen people who chose to handle a financial blessing that obviously came from God in such a way that the blessing became the storm that brought their house down. I have come to the conclusion that many of the struggles believers go through, many of the problems and weaknesses we experience, and even many of those things we consider attacks from the enemy can be traced back to a weak spiritual foundation.

Most believers have what could be described as isolated experiences with God. Very few experience consistent, unbroken, and systematic spiritual development and growth. Very few follow a well-designed set of blueprints or plans for spiritual growth, tending instead to get a little bit of God here and a little bit of God there. Many follow God for several years, fall away, and then come back and find themselves starting over. In the process of building their spiritual houses, they complete some of the work in a hurry, do some of it wrong, and leave some of it undone. Meanwhile, a storm is coming.

What God says to us in this parable is simply this: "Let's stop for a moment and check the foundation. If it's strong enough for what I want to build on it, then I will check off the permit. If not, let's repair it, finish it, and do whatever needs to be done to make it strong enough to survive the storms of life."

Are We Building the Right Foundation?

In addition to making certain we're building a strong foundation, we also need to know that we are building the right foundation. Paul talks about this in 1 Corinthians 3:11: "For no one can lay any foundation other than the one already laid, which is Jesus Christ."

Often we try to build our spiritual life on a certain church tradition or denominational background, on church attendance or church membership, or on a certain doctrine or practice, such as baptism, confirmation, or Communion. Not uncommonly, we attempt to build our spiritual life on someone else's relationship with God, such as that of a spouse, parent, or best friend. None of these things are bad in themselves; they just aren't the right foundation on which to build our spiritual life. We simply cannot build a spiritual life unless there is the foundation of a personal relationship with Jesus Christ.

The Bible teaches that salvation is available only through the person of Jesus Christ. No other way makes us right with God except placing our faith in Jesus Christ and in his death and resurrection. Acts 4:12 tells us, "Salvation is found in no one else, for there is no other name under heaven given to men by which we must be saved." Salvation is available only through a faith relationship with Jesus Christ.

The Bible also tells us that to enter into that relationship, we must be born again. When we place our faith in Christ for salvation, a spiritual change

15

takes place. Spiritually speaking, we become new persons. This transformation is not imaginary or psychologically induced, nor is it merely wishful thinking; it is as real as natural birth.

When we have a faith relationship with Jesus Christ, we become new persons, and as a result, our lives change. We see things in a different way and understand things we've never understood before. We feel different about ourselves and about life, because something has changed on the inside. All of life is different. It's like being born again!

Until we have been born again, we simply can't know God. We can have opinions about God, but those opinions are probably wrong because they're based on human understanding and perspective and not upon spiritual reality. To have spiritual perspective we must have new eyes and a new mind, and to get new eyes and a new mind, we must be born again. This is how we ensure that we are building on the right foundation.

IS OUR FOUNDATION COMPLETE?

Not only do we want to be sure that we are building a strong foundation and the right foundation, but we also want to be sure we build a complete foundation.

This is where Hebrews 6:1–3 becomes especially important to us, because it identifies critical elements that need to be in place in the foundation of our spiritual life. This passage tells us to leave the basics of our faith and press on to maturity, "not laying again the foundation"; it then lists six very specific aspects of our relationship with Christ that form our foundation:

- Repentance from acts that lead to death (*dead works*)
- Faith in God
- Instruction about baptisms
- Laying on of hands
- The resurrection of the dead
- Eternal judgment

Each of these six foundational stones represents a specific way in which God releases an identifiable measure of grace into our lives, providing something for us that we are unable to provide for ourselves. As I mentioned previously, the essence of the grace-based life is learning to let God do for us those things that we are unable to do for ourselves and to provide for us those things we are unable to provide for ourselves. When the spiritual truth contained in these six foundational stones become real to us and produce what God designed them to produce, they release specific measures of grace that become foundational in our relationship with Christ.

Repentance from Dead Works

This foundation stone of repentance from dead works releases the grace we need in order to quit trying so hard to make ourselves acceptable to God. It turns us toward what God has provided for us

17

through the sacrificial life and death of Jesus as the means by which we become righteous and are able to have a relationship with Him.

Faith in God

This foundation stone releases the grace necessary to trust God. Before we come to know God, we tend to be afraid of Him, uncertain how He feels about us. We are not sure whether He is a good God who is *for* us or whether He is waiting for us to make a mistake so He can crush us like a bug. The grace released though faith in God helps us see the character of God; that He truly is a good God who is for us.

Instruction about Baptisms

This foundation stone gives us grace for the race. Each of the four baptisms mentioned in Scripture is designed to release the spiritual resources needed to turn theory into the kind of firsthand experience that becomes unshakeable, foundational truth in our life and enables us to finish our race in strength.

The *baptism of repentance* in Luke 3:3 releases the grace that gives us the willingness to be changed. *Water baptism* frees us from the penalty and power of sin (Rom. 6:3–7), while the *baptism of fire* referred to in Matthew 3:11 releases the grace we need in order to surrender our will to God's will for us. The *baptism of the Holy Spirit* (Acts 1:8) enables us to know the Spirit of God as the power of God.

Laying On of Hands

This foundation stone allows us to live a blessed life with clear evidence of the favor of God.

The Resurrection of the Dead

This foundation stone means that because of God's grace, every area of our life that is subject to death can be restored to life.

Eternal Judgment

The final stone in the foundation is eternal judgment, which releases the grace necessary to choose wisely as we consider the choices and options that we face in life.

Together these six foundation stones create the type of foundation upon which you can build a grace-based life, because as God releases the truth and spiritual provision of each of these six foundation stones into your life, you'll be building on the most solid foundation of all, a foundation of grace. This grace has many aspects, which we will now explore.

CHAPTER 3

THE GRACE TO QUIT TRYING SO HARD

I WAS EXPERIENCING one of those moments that leaves its mark on your soul. The young man sitting across from me was about my own age and had just been released from a mental hospital in our city, where he had been treated for a nervous breakdown. As we sat and got acquainted, I understood the reason for his struggles. Extremely serious about God and deeply concerned about his salvation, he felt emotional pressure as a result of those two concerns, and that pressure caused his problems.

According to his religious tradition and understanding, his own efforts and goodness—rather than what God had done for him—determined God's acceptance of him and subsequently his salvation. He was probably the most dramatic case I ever met of someone who needed to repent from dead works.

A list of do's and don'ts and the uncertainty of not knowing when he had done enough to be right with God governed his whole life. Fear caused by uncertainty had led to his nervous breakdown; he literally had driven himself to the point of emotional collapse by trying so hard to get right with God.

I was never able to help him understand that salvation is God's gift, made possible by grace and faith. The last I heard of him, he had returned to the hospital with continuing emotional struggles.

When it comes to establishing and maintaining a relationship with God, most of us don't reach the point of despair of this young man, but many of us—believers included—go through life depending more on self-effort than we do on God's grace. Like this young man, our greatest need is to quit trying so hard and let God do for us what we are trying to do through our own efforts. We need to be set free from the "dead works" approach to God and learn to enjoy the salvation available through grace and faith.

In this chapter we will look at several specific aspects of repentance from dead works, the first stone in the foundation of the grace-based life. First, we will define a dead work. Then we will examine what makes it a dead work. Finally, we will look at what happens in our lives as we begin to live in the grace that enables us to quit trying so hard and let God provide for us what we are unable to provide for ourselves.

WHAT IS A DEAD WORK?

Salvation begins with a question: how do we become acceptable to God? Every person who has ever lived has asked this question in one form or another. Ecclesiastes 3:11 tells us that God has "set eternity in hearts of men," which indicates that we are made for more than just this life and at the same time are motivated by an inner hunger to discover the fuller meaning of our existence. It is in the search for that fuller meaning of life that we begin to think in terms of God or a higher being.

The problem is that we also have a built-in awareness that in order for us to have a relationship with God, something has to change. Deep down we know we are not acceptable as we are—that we need to be cleaned up in some way. We also know we don't have enough to offer. Something is missing, and we must find it before we become acceptable to God.

Who does the cleaning up? Do I clean up myself, or does God have to do it? Who provides what is missing? Do I provide it, or does God supply it for me? When we don't understand the concept of faith and grace, we come to the conclusion that we have to do it ourselves. We decide we have to provide what is lacking and clean ourselves up before we become acceptable to God. Any attempt to make ourselves acceptable to God by what we do or don't do is what the Bible refers to as a dead work.

Dead works focus on self-effort, and therein lies the problem. Don't play cards. Don't go to movies. Don't dance, but do go to church. Stop cussing, stop smoking, and stop drinking. Don't chew, and certainly don't go with girls who do. Then surely God will like us better. He might even find us acceptable. People who don't understand faith and grace often think this way.

However, doing or not doing certain things does not make us acceptable to God.

THE DEAD-WORKS APPROACH

When it comes to salvation, what we do or don't do always ends in failure, for several reasons.

First of all, the dead-works approach to making ourselves acceptable to God fails to deal with our real need. I am talking about the difference between sin and sins. When we hear the word *sin*, we often actually think in terms of *sins*, and that's what moves us toward dead works.

To understand the difference between sin and sins, think of it this way. Sin is a spiritual condition. Applying this idea to the natural side of life, we could say that sin is like having a cold or the flu. It's a condition. Sins, on the other hand, are *symptoms* of our condition. When we have a cold, we experience certain symptoms, including sneezing, a running nose, or a sore throat. The spiritual condition of sin also causes certain symptoms—sins—including jealousy, lustful thoughts, stealing, and lying. These actions are symptoms of the spiritual condition of sin.

Sin (the condition)—not our sins (the symptoms)—makes us unacceptable to God. Here's the issue: *Sins* will certainly damage our relationship with God once it is established, but *sin* prevents that relationship in the first place. Until we do something about our spiritual condition, we have no relationship to damage.

We must remember that what we are—not what we do or don't do—is what makes us unacceptable to God. Although we most often focus on controlling or changing the symptoms (particular sins), breaking free from the condition of sin comprises our greatest need. Dead works result from our attempts to control or change the symptoms.

TREAT THE CONDITION, NOT THE SYMPTOMS

Symptoms don't keep us from God; our sinful condition does. That's why you must be born again. When you are born again, your condition changes—you become a new creation in Christ, and once your condition changes, you are acceptable to God. When you are born again, Christ provides you with garments of righteousness to replace your garments of unrighteousness. When you put on His righteousness, God declares you acceptable, all because He has done for you what you were unable to do for yourself. Your condition changes because of grace.

To repent from dead works, we must quit putting our attention on the symptoms. Our problem is our condition, and we can't do anything about that except trust God to change it for us. God created us, and through the miracle of rebirth, He will re-create us. We become new creations in Christ because of what God has provided and done for us.

The inability of the dead-works approach to deal with the real issue is not the only reason to turn from it. It also has a negative effect on the kind of persons we become as believers.

When we try to use the dead-works approach to make ourselves acceptable to God, we tend to turn into abnormal, strange creatures, robbed of our natural human traits and morphed into religious caricatures who come across as laughable at best and absurd at worst. In other words, we tend to start acting religious, displaying a poor substitute for authentic spirituality. Dead works keep us from being ourselves.

Let me give you an example. What do you do when someone tells an inappropriate but funny joke? Do you laugh or rebuke? I am not suggesting you should laugh, but I am saying if you think that by not laughing you are somehow more acceptable to God, you are using a dead-works approach to spirituality. It won't work.

I am convinced that the more authentically spiritual people become, the more natural and human they also become. By this I don't mean they become carnal and develop an attitude of carelessness about sin, but they feel free to be who God created them to be.

Normal and Natural

One of the reasons Jesus found such favor with many sinners and common ordinary people, I believe, is that He was like them in the sense that He was normal and natural. It was the Pharisees, the religious-acting people, who had such problems with Him. Jesus tends to make people who are focused on self-effort nervous.

Have you ever wondered what Jesus' disciples talked about when they were together? We know from Scripture they discussed things like the kingdom of God and other related subjects, but what about the times they spent together that are not recorded in Scripture? What did they talk about during those times?

I think they probably talked about sports, politics, or maybe what it would be like to be rich. I know many people couldn't care less about such things, and that's OK; I am not suggesting that you have to like football, for example. But I am saying that if you think that not liking football makes you more spiritual than those who do, you are missing the whole concept. What you like or don't like doesn't make you spiritual and thus acceptable to God; it's what Jesus has done for us that makes it possible to be spiritual.

In other words, I think Jesus' disciples were normal, natural people who felt free to be themselves when they were with Jesus, and I think that as they grew spiritually they remained natural, normal people with human reactions and emotions.

How do you think Peter and John responded the day Peter prayed for a crippled man and the man was healed (Acts 3:1–6)? I don't think Peter responded in a somber, churchy voice, "It's not me, it's the Lord. I am only the vessel." I think Peter and John saw the man jumping around in excitement and turned to each other and said, "Yes, high five, dude!" I think that even though they were thrilled at the sight of the healed man, they were probably still as amazed that God used them in such a way as they were the first time He used them in that way and that they reacted with a normal human reaction. But if Peter and John had used the dead-works approach to God, they would have felt led to quit their jobs and start healing ministries—probably on TV—and eventually they would have become some type of weird, unnatural caricatures of humanity who conveyed the message, "This is what you have to do to be acceptable to God."

When we think we have to act a certain way to be acceptable to God, we tend to act religious. Acting religious and doing dead works makes a deadly combination. People like this simply do not deal with the real issue or create authentic spirituality, and that's why we need to turn in repentance from both behaviors.

TURNING FROM DEAD WORKS

There is, however, an even more compelling reason to turn from the dead-works approach to being right with God: dead works don't prepare us for the way of the Lord in our life.

When we are faced with a problem or need, we have to find a way to meet that need, and we have two options. First, we can follow the way of the Lord, which is based on grace and produces true spirituality. Alternatively, we can follow the way of dead works, which is based on self-effort and leads to spiritual failure and exhaustion—a result of trying so hard we wear ourselves out.

To turn from dead works, you must quit trying so hard to make yourself acceptable, which is man's way. Stop the self-effort and follow the way of grace, allowing God to do for you what you can't do for yourself and to provide for you what you can't provide for yourself. Quit trying so hard to make yourself acceptable, and let God do it for you. Place your faith in Jesus Christ as your Savior. Remember, Jesus can't be your Savior if you are going to try to be your own savior.

Now let's look at the next stone in our foundation—faith in God. In the next chapter we will discover how to escape the pressure of trying to "have faith" by learning to have faith in God.

CHAPTER 4

THE GRACE TO HAVE FAITH IN GOD

H ER NAME WAS Amy. She was as beautiful on the inside as she was on the outside, and at twenty-six, she was much too young to die, but she did.

For almost a year, our church, along with literally thousands of people at intercessors conferences, churches in our area, and places throughout the world, prayed that God would heal her of the cancer stealing her life. We all knew He could, and we had hoped beyond hope that He would, but now she was gone, and the question on everyone's mind was, Why didn't God answer our prayer?

I will never forget standing in the pulpit and facing the congregation on the first Sunday after her death. I fought to hold back my tears as I sought the words that needed to be said that morning. "As you all know," I began, "Amy passed away this week, and I know we're all sitting here wondering why. Why didn't God heal her? Why didn't He answer our prayers? I want to be sensitive in how I say this, but all I know to say is that He did answer our prayers. He said no. His answer was no."

There was not one person sitting there that morning who had not at some time and in some way asked God to heal Amy, but He didn't. He had in fact said no, and we were left wondering what that meant. What did it say about us? What did it say about God? What did it say about our faith? These are questions I want to look at in this chapter.

We need to begin by understanding the difference between "having faith" and having faith in God. There is a subtle but distinct difference between the two concepts, and we need to know that difference in those moments when God says no or when things are not working the way we think they should. "Having faith" is not the foundation stone referred to in Hebrews 6. That passage is referring to faith in God or faith that is foundational, and there is considerable difference between that and "having faith." Not everything we in the body of Christ identify as faith is actually foundational faith, strong enough to stand in the face of the storms of life and to support whatever God wants to build on it. In fact, I am convinced that what many identify as faith is actually a dead work and not a living, vital faith in God.

CHARACTERISTICS OF FAITH AS A DEAD WORK

Sometimes we attempt to provide or produce a spiritual result through self-effort and call this "having faith." This often results in disastrous situations that can actually cause significant damage to existing faith.

When we see faith as a way of using God to achieve a personal goal or fulfill a personal desire, we have probably moved into the realm of dead works. Faith becomes a force that God simply cannot resist, a spiritual force stronger than God himself. Of course it follows that if we have enough faith, we can get God to do whatever we want Him to do. Therein lies the danger! At first glance this appealing concept may seem right, but the test of its validity comes in the times when God says no or when things don't happen the way we pray.

The failure of this type of faith leaves us with a serious question. What does it mean when God says no or when things are not working out the way we hoped or imagined? Does it mean that those who prayed didn't pray in faith or didn't have enough faith? That's usually the first thing that comes to mind at a moment like this: *If I just had more faith, this wouldn't have happened.*

In reality, thinking this way can lead us to certain false conclusions, which in turn can lead to disastrous results as we fail to recognize one of the significant dangers associated with faith. That danger has to do with the fine line between asking in faith when we pray and attempting to use our prayers of faith as a way of manipulating or forcing God to do what we want Him to do.

I want to be very careful not to dampen anyone's efforts to walk in faith, but at the same time I want to say that faith should never be presented as a means by which we are able to control God as we would a puppet on a string. Faith is not a means by which we force God into action. We must not view it as something so powerful that God himself cannot resist it, that He in fact becomes a slave to our faith as its sheer strength compels Him to obey our desires. I get concerned about this approach to faith, but I am even more concerned about the damage that can come through doubt and condemnation because of the subtle suggestion that if we just had more faith, or if we had used a certain formula, this wouldn't have happened.

Let me share a couple of simple ways to know when we are demonstrating faith in God.

The very act of praying expresses faith in God. An incident recorded in Acts 12:6–19 illustrates this. Peter had been put in jail, and the church was concerned about what to do when apparently someone suggested that maybe they should pray. They did begin to pray, and a short time later Peter, who had been freed from prison by an angel, was knocking on the door. We need to notice their response of absolute surprise and disbelief, which indicates to me that they did not start that prayer meeting with a great deal of faith. But they did have enough faith to pray.

In a second incident (Matt. 15:21–28), Matthew tells the story of a woman who came to Jesus with a significant need. At first the Lord and his disciples ignored her, but she kept asking until her request was heard. Jesus interpreted her persistence as an expression of faith.

The question is not whether we have perfect faith, with no doubt ever evident in our hearts. Rather we should examine whether we have prayed about the things that concern us and continued to share our hearts with God about those concerns. If we have, then true faith was both active and present in our prayers. If God does say no, it simply means His answer was no; it doesn't mean we were not praying in faith.

You see, the enemy would like to use the idea that we don't have enough faith to keep us from believing and from pressing God the next time we face a similar situation. He wants to use God's no to develop in us a what's-the-use mentality and convince us there's no reason to pray, since we obviously don't have enough faith.

Don't let God's no derail your faith. Sometimes His answer is just no.

Does No Mean God Doesn't Care?

Let's ask another question about those times when God says no. Does no from God mean He didn't hear us or doesn't care about us?

3 5

Many years ago our oldest son needed some medical procedures, and we took him to a clinic. When we got there, the nurses took him from us and carried him to a room where the procedures would be done. Shortly after they began, he decided to express his displeasure with a very loud and verbal explanation of how he felt about it.

We were only a few doors away and could hear him clearly. Everything in our hearts as his mom and dad wanted to go rescue him, to respond to his cries for help, but we didn't. When our son called to us, we said no. Our son couldn't understand the reason we didn't answer him. If you had asked him, "Did your mom and dad hear you when you cried for help?" he might have said, "Well, apparently they didn't hear me or care, because they didn't do what I was asking them to do. They didn't come to my rescue." But the truth is, we did hear him, loud and clear. We refused to help him because his discomfort served a larger purpose, and we did not want to interfere with that purpose.

I certainly do not know God perfectly, but I do know this: God always hears the prayers of His people. Sometimes He just says no, and when He does, it doesn't mean He turned a deaf ear to the heart cry, the pain, or the desires being expressed through the prayers of those calling out to Him. It only means He doesn't always respond the way we would prefer or always answer the way we ask. It means He sometimes says no because He is working out a greater purpose in our life.

Does No Mean God Broke His Promise?

Now let's look at another question that often troubles people during those times and situations when God says no.

When God says no, does that mean He broke His promise, that He didn't fulfill the word He gave us about the situation? Many times we feel that God has spoken to us about the situation, and if it doesn't happen the way we thought it was going to, we find ourselves with a shaken confidence in God and in our own spiritual ability. This can be tough, but we need to develop the spiritual skill of distinguishing between the general promises of God found in His Word and the way they relate to our specific situation.

What we are really talking about here is the difference between *logos* and *rhema*, the difference between the general and the specific. *Logos* is the general Word of God; it is everything God says about a subject or an area of life. As a practical matter, we can think of the Bible as the Logos of God. It is His complete revelation given in a general way. *Rhema*, on the other hand, is the specific word He speaks to us about our specific situation. The *logos* becomes *rhema* when the Holy Spirit takes something out of the general Word and makes it alive to us in our specific area of need. *Rhema* is the personalized version of *logos*. It is when God, whom we know as a healing God, speaks to our spirit that He is going to heal us of our specific need. When that happens, faith is birthed in our spirit, and we move from believing or wanting God to do something to knowing He is going to do what we are requesting Him to do.

The problem is that much of our prayer is focused on appealing to the general Word—the promise, the *logos*—and while there is nothing inherently wrong with that, it can lead to problems if He says no and we interpret that as Him breaking His promise or word to us.

When He says no, it doesn't mean He broke His promise. It probably means that we did not have a *rhema*, a specific word from God about our specific situation, and that we had a strong desire to see the *logos* apply to our situation but did not have a "personalized promise" given us by the Holy Spirit.

I may be wrong, but I believe that when we get the *rhema* we have no further need to pray in the same way. In fact, I believe that when we receive the *rhema* of God about our situation, we are through asking, and it's time to move to the praise phase of our prayer. *Rhema* is a word that is alive in our spirit, something that tells us this is a done deal and now it's time to say, "Thank you, Lord, for what you have done."

At that point we are not focused on believing that God can do what needs to be done. The focus changes to the spiritual reality in our spirit that *knows* what He is going to do.

Trust in the Sovereignty of God

So what underlying issue must we face at those times when God says no? What lesson does God want to build into our relationship with Him that we will need for the journey we are on? Without a doubt, I believe that the issue at stake is the issue of trust. Not blind, passive trust that asks no questions but trust anchored in the sovereignty of God.

If you don't take away anything else from what I'm saying here, get this point: you will never get to a place in your relationship with God where you no longer need to trust in His sovereignty.

Trusting in the sovereignty of God brings peace to those storms in life when we know He could have said yes but He chose to say no. Trusting in the sovereignty of God means finding peace between what we know He can do and what He chose not to do. This kind of trust believes when God says yes and believes still when he says no.

Trusting in the sovereignty of God is not the expression of a passive resignation whereby we give in to some obscure concept of fate. Trusting in the sovereignty of God is an active expression of faith based on a heart-level conviction that

- God's timing is right.
- God's ways are right.
- God's purpose is right.

Trusting in the sovereignty of God answers the charge the enemy would like to lodge against the name, character, and goodness of God.

Trusting in the sovereignty of God is Jesus in the garden saying, "Take this cup from me; yet not my will, but yours be done (Luke 22:42).

It's Job standing in the midst of all that has collapsed around him and declaring, "Though he slay me, yet will I trust in him" (Job 13:15 KJV).

It's children of God standing in the face of overwhelming challenges, refusing to let go of our conviction that "neither death nor life, neither angels nor demons, neither the present nor the future, nor any powers, neither height nor depth, nor anything else in all creation, will be able to separate us from the love of God that is in Christ Jesus our Lord" (Rom. 8:38–39), because in our heart we have learned that "in all these things we are more than conquerors through him who loved us" (v. 37).

Trust in the sovereignty of God. Learn to move through those times when God says no by focusing on His greatness, love, and impacting purposes being worked out in your life.

FAITH IN GOD AS FOUNDATIONAL FAITH

The story of Abraham and Sarah's hope for a baby provides probably the best illustration of faith in God as foundational faith. At the age of one hundred and ninety, respectively, their childbearing years were at best a distant memory, but because they had faith in God and not just faith for a miracle pregnancy, God's no became God's yes in their lives. Let's look at how that happened.

The Bible tells us that the progress toward this miracle birth began when Abraham faced the fact that his body and Sarah's womb were as good as dead. In other words, these two didn't have much to offer in the fulfillment of their dream, and they both knew it. They knew they were not going to be able to bring much to the party, but that didn't keep them from going to the party!

Foundational faith starts with an honest assessment of the situation we face, as opposed to playing some mind game complete with religious-sounding overtones. Abraham didn't say, "I am going to claim the body of a bodybuilder by faith." He didn't say, "I'm not really one hundred years old." He faced the fact that he was one hundred years old and that when it came to the reproductive act, his body was as good as dead.

I believe that until you make an honest assessment of your situation and, like Abraham, face facts, you may try to fix things yourself and thus move into dead works. After an honest assessment, you may instead realize that any solution is beyond your ability. You realize that unless God acts, everything is going to be lost. There's nothing to have faith for or have faith about.

It seems to me that we must make an honest assessment of our situation as the starting place for faith. The realization of our helplessness primes the pump of faith. When we acknowledge that this situation will require a miracle—which can only come from God—we focus on Him and give faith an opportunity to develop. For problems we can handle ourselves, we have no need to release faith.

As I mentioned before, foundational faith is also based on God's promise to you regarding your situation. Again, Abraham shows us the way. Even after he had made an honest assessment of his situation and realized its desperate nature, he did not waver through unbelief regarding the promise that God would give him a son. Although he didn't know how it would work out or how God would make it possible, Abraham didn't let go of the promise.

I have come to understand that faith never stands alone; it always occurs in association or relation to something else, most commonly with the Word of God. Abraham had a word from God. God had told him he was going to be the father of a child, and the facts surrounding the case didn't shake his faith in that promise.

Without a word from God regarding our situation, we lack the raw material for foundational faith, and the Holy Spirit has nothing to work with in bringing that word into reality. When God personalizes one of His promises for us, it becomes a foundational reality and we can stand on it through all types of challenges and obstacles.

When Jeanne and I started in ministry, we were young, insecure, and inexperienced in what we were called to do. I lacked the internal courage to lead the church, and in reality I walked in the fear of man until one day God personalized one of his promises for me. One morning during my struggle with some of the opposition I encountered in the church, I turned to the passage in Revelation 3:8 where Jesus says, "I have placed before you an open door that no one can shut." The words came alive to me and became one of my first experiences with the personalized promises of God. The promise became foundational to me, and over the next twenty-one years of ministry in that place, I stood on that promise whenever the storms came. Foundational faith is always connected to the personalized promises God has whispered into our soul.

We need to understand another aspect of foundational faith—that faith is released and established in our hearts to the degree we are convinced that God not only has the ability to do what needs to be done in our situation, but that He desires to use His ability for us. Even when we believe that God can do anything, we often find it very difficult to accept the idea that He wants to do something for us. We have trouble accepting the reality that God is for us, not against us. When we correct that misconception, faith begins to ooze out of the pores of our souls, and we begin to live the grace-based life.

This is the opposite of faith as a dead work. There's no room in this for self-effort or for achieving something by using God as a personal servant. This is a different approach than creating a wish list or a to-do list for God. This isn't about "having faith." It's about having faith in God. It's faith based on trust, which gives us the ability to surrender our situation to God's plan and purpose. It's saying, "God, I have a situation here that needs you. You're the only one who can do anything about it or change it. I know you can, and I am asking you to do that for me, but no matter how it turns out, I will still know that you are a good God and that you are for me."

That's foundational faith, not "having faith" but rather having faith in God. "Having faith" focuses on the power of God and the results that can be achieved because of that power, whereas having faith in God puts the emphasis on the character, nature, and motives of God, which is the very essence of trust. Without this type of foundational faith, we will not have what we need to stand in the face of the storms of life or to support what God wants to build in our lives. When we don't have a personalized promise of God for our situation, we had better be able to trust God himself, because without that we will fall when the results are not what we want or during those times when God says no.

Are you struggling to "have faith" for some situation? You risk ending up in condemnation or cynicism when you are not able to produce the faith you seek. Quit trying to "have faith" and decide instead to trust God's character, His nature, and His willingness to do what fulfills His purpose for your life. In other words, what you need is the foundation stone of having faith in God.

But what if you haven't been able to move to a place where you truly are standing on a foundation of faith in God? What does God need to do for you to enable you to make that change?

The parable of the talents in Matthew 25:14–30 illustrates how you need God to release His grace in your life. In this story the master gives three people the opportunity to develop and fulfill their destiny: the ten-talent man, the five-talent man, and the one-talent man. The first two had no trouble living up to the possibilities presented to them. They took what they had been given and made the most of it, but the one-talent man encountered a significant roadblock on his journey—the image he had of his master. He saw the master as "a hard man," which affected the nature of their relationship. "I knew that you are a hard man . . . . I was afraid and went out and hid your talent in the ground."

A wrong image always leads to a wrong relationship, which in turn produces a wrong result.

CHAPTER 5

THE GRACE TO TURN THEORY INTO FIRSTHAND EXPERIENCE

HOW WOULD YOU describe your spiritual development at this point in your journey? Would you say you have lived more in the realm of theory or more in the realm of firsthand experience? If you were asked to share how your relationship with Jesus has changed your life, what would you say? What obstacles have you overcome because of God's work in you and your life situation? What has become so real to you that it has become foundational in your life?

This chapter will discuss turning theory into firsthand experience. It may surprise you that the grace we need comes through our next foundation stone, instruction about baptisms.

When most people hear the term *baptism*, they normally think of water baptism, and while water baptism relates to this discussion, thinking only of water baptism misses what makes instruction about baptisms foundational in our spiritual life. You might be surprised to discover that the Bible mentions four distinct situations as baptisms, which is why this foundation stone is called instruction about baptisms.

We must fight the temptation to focus on water baptism (and perhaps also the baptism of the Holy Spirit) and then feel that we have this foundation stone firmly in place, moving right on to the next one. I believe that approach misses the real issue. We need to answer two questions: What measure of grace does God release into our life when this particular foundation stone takes its proper place? What makes baptisms foundational in our spiritual development?

Total Immersion, the Foundational Concept

The Greek word for baptism is *baptizo*, which implies a total immersion into some form of fluid or liquid. For that reason, many Christian traditions use immersion in water as their form of baptism. Please don't get hung up at this point about what method should be used. This discussion is not about methods of baptism; it's about moving from theory into the realm of firsthand experience in some critical areas of life.

Having said that, let me suggest to you the idea of total immersion as key to understanding how instruction about baptisms is part of our spiritual foundation.

In the Scriptures we find four distinct situations referred to as baptisms:

- Baptism of repentance (Luke 3:3)
- Water baptism (Rom. 6:3–7)
- Baptism of fire (Matt. 3:11)
- Baptism of the Holy Spirit (Acts 1:8)

I think each of these four baptisms represents a measure of grace we need in order to overcome specific obstacles we will encounter on our journey. Throughout Scripture we find the call to fight a good fight, to finish the race, and to remain faithful to the end. Each of these admonitions suggests the idea of coming to the end of our race in spiritual strength, still gaining momentum as we approach the finish line. They suggest someone who is not coasting to the finish on yesterday's experiences with God but is continuing to grow in depth of spirit and soul and in a greater revelation of God in a personal and firsthand way.

Actually, the idea found in Scripture is the opposite of what happens in the lives of many of God's people. At some point many believers slip into neutral and begin coasting to the finish line. They consider finishing the race more an act of survival than a moment of victory.

I believe that if we come to the end of our race with little spiritual strength left, we had never learned to keep our spiritual reservoir filled with the grace released into our life through a total-immersion experience—the experience that establishes us in the spiritual truths represented by each of the four baptisms. In other words, we run out of strength before we reach the finish line because throughout our spiritual journey we avoided a total-immersion experience—a baptism—in these four areas in a way that would have made it foundational in our life.

All believers encounter certain key obstacles that have the power to keep us from finishing in strength and victory. To overcome these obstacles, we need grace. We need God to do for us what we are unable to do for ourselves so that the obstacles won't overcome our progress and development.

The obstacles we face correspond to the four baptisms mentioned in Scripture:

- The baptism of repentance is about opening ourselves to being changed.
- Water baptism is about a new identity and freedom from the power of sin.
- The baptism of fire is about surrendering our will to His will.
- Holy Spirit baptism is about knowing the Spirit of God as the power of God.

We will look at each of these obstacles in turn.

Being Willing or Unable to Change or Be Changed

Every one of us has probably met one of those hard, crusty old persons who are unpleasant to be around. Usually we explain their behavior by saying they have become senile, but I am not sure that's always accurate. Many times a self-centered, cranky old person is simply a self-centered ten-year-old who never changed, who was self-focused at ten and is still self-focused at eighty-five.

Because most of us want to be thought of as nice people, we learn early to control some of our less-than-pleasant tendencies, but as we reach a place in life where we are less concerned with what others think of us, some of those tendencies might begin to surface. When that happens, it is evident that very little real change ever took place; that we are still the self-focused person we were as a child.

The grace of God at work in our lives results in real change. In a sense, change becomes the evidence that the God who created us is re-creating us and making us more like His Son, Jesus.

Not Overcoming the Power of Sin

In the same vein, I have seen some very respectable people—people whom many would consider poster children for God—suddenly do something that no one could explain, something that in effect destroyed the influence of their good lives as well as the happiness of their remaining years. A seemingly godly grandparent inexplicably abuses a grandchild.

A senior decides to leave a marriage partner of fifty years for someone else. A couple spends their life savings on some worthless venture and ends up struggling to survive financially. How are we to explain these strange and unreasonable behaviors?

If it were possible to get all the facts in many situations like those I have just described, we would discover that these people had struggled with a particular area of sin throughout their lives and were never able to overcome it. Suddenly the sin expressed itself in some shocking and unexplainable way.

We need to understand the patience of Satan. He doesn't care if he wins today or has to wait until a later time. He just wants to win, and tomorrow is as good as today. Whether he knocks us out in the third round or the tenth is of little importance to him. He just wants to knock us out. He will lie in wait for years, watching us ignore a specific area of sin throughout our lives, and then in a moment when we are weak, tempted, and vulnerable from coasting in spiritual neutral, Satan will act. He will use our unconquered sin to do as much damage as possible. It seems that later-in-life failures do greater damage than failures earlier in life. When a young person yields to the power of sin, it is a difficult and damaging dynamic, but when grandpa or grandma does the same thing, the sin has a much more far-reaching and destructive influence.

The lesson we can learn from these tragic moments is that each of us needs to walk in grace—letting God do for us those things we are unable to do for ourselves—at each stage and season of life.

Finding It Difficult to Surrender to God's Will

Most of us learn at an early age that it is easier to receive forgiveness than it is to get permission. We are confident that if we say, "Mom, I'm sorry I didn't get home on time," mom will forgive us, but we are not as confident that she will give us permission to stay at our friend's house later than usual. Unfortunately, this mentality can be carried over into another aspect of our relationship with God, that of surrendering to His will for our lives.

As a pastor, I have been approached by many people who wondered why they were not experiencing more of God's blessing in their lives, why they seemed continually to run into an invisible wall of resistance that frustrated their efforts to move successfully through the seasons and stages of life. After I asked a few questions, the problem often became apparent—they had never come to the place in their relationships with God where His will for them became the priority. They decided what they wanted to do, asked God to bless their plans, and then wondered what was wrong with Him when He didn't.

The Bible tells us that God will never forsake us or leave us, but it does not say that He has an obligation to pour His resources, power, and blessing into our plans. He is obligated only to do His will. His will always receives a full measure of His resources, power, and blessing. If you find these spiritual elements missing in your life situation and wonder why God doesn't seem interested in blessing your attempts at life, maybe you need to go back and examine your approach to life. Rather than starting with your plans and asking God to bless them, start with the simple question, "Lord, what is your will for me?" Why not make that small adjustment to your relationship with God and see what happens?

Not Knowing the Holy Spirit as the Power of God

Somehow the role of the Holy Spirit became a controversial subject in Christian circles, and the result led to many frustrated believers attempting to live the Christian life through their own strength and power. We often know the Holy Spirit more in theory than as the power of God in our lives. In reality, the Christian life cannot be lived successfully without the Holy Spirit's help. Limiting and restricting the Holy Spirit's activity in our lives will almost guarantee that we won't finish the race in victory.

The Holy Spirit is the creative expression of God, and when we lack certain abilities and spiritual skills, the Holy Spirit creates those things in our lives—things like courage, endurance, and peace. The Holy Spirit uses the circumstances of life as well as our cooperation to begin the creative process in us.

If you want to finish your journey with the Lord, you must learn to know the Spirit of God as the power of God. Then you will cross the finish line in victory.

WHAT MAKES THE FOUR BAPTISMS FOUNDATIONAL?

The four obstacles we just examined can keep us from finishing our race, and as I mentioned earlier, they correspond to the four baptisms of Scripture. These four baptisms become foundational in believers' lives when God totally immerses us in some experience or encounter with Him to the degree that we move out of the realm of theory and into the realm of firsthand experience and knowledge with Him and about Him.

For example, a baptism—a total-immersion encounter—with the Holy Spirit takes the power and reality of God's Spirit out of the realm of theory. When that happens, the Holy Spirit is no longer simply a theory, a comforting idea, a concept, or a doctrine that we believe. The Holy Spirit becomes a person with whom we've had tangible, firsthand experience, and what we know from experience cannot be shaken; it becomes foundational in our life.

There are some aspects of my relationship with God that have never been totally immersed, even though I believe. On the other hand, some have been established in my life through experience. The latter have become foundational—unshakeable—to me. One still exists as a belief in my life while the other is established as a firsthand experience in which I was totally immersed by some situation or season with God. One I believe is true, and one I know is true because I have experienced it. The person with the experience is never at the mercy of the person with the theory.

Let me touch briefly on three moments that introduced me to the concept of total immersion as a tool through which God turns theory into firsthand, foundational truth.

A Father's Heart

The first was the birth of our oldest son. Jeanne and I didn't plan on being the parents of a special-needs child; we were just fortunate enough to be allowed to be. It was through our son that I learned the importance of embracing those moments that have the potential of bringing brokenness into our lives.

Treg is a brain-damaged young man who was born addicted to drugs because his birth mother was a fourteen-year-old girl who had used drugs extensively. When we adopted Treg, we discovered that in addition to the limitations brought about by his retardation, we had to accept the reality and challenge of dealing with the symptoms of his addiction.

The biggest single issue was the sleep problems that were part of his condition. For three-and-a-half years, Treg woke up screaming approximately every forty-five minutes and would have to be rocked back to sleep. In a state of constant exhaustion, we learned how to deal with the confusion, disappointment, and pain of our child's handicap.

For me, it all came to a head one day when I was talking to God about the situation. I had been struggling with the difficulty of living with my own pain—made more challenging because as a pastor I had to do so before the whole church. So did my wife. Neither one of us could go away and hide as we wanted to. We shed our tears in public.

As I sat there that morning, I said, "God, I don't understand why he was born this way. Why did he have to be this way?" Then as God often does, He whispered to my soul and said, "All I did was answer your prayer."

I responded in anger. If I could have gotten my hands around God's throat, I would have choked him. I felt like He was mocking me in my pain. *Answer my prayer? What prayer?* my heart demanded. *I never prayed to have a retarded son.*

"That's not what I am talking about," came the response inside. "Remember when you asked me to give you a father's heart? You need to understand, son, you can't have a father's heart until you've had a broken heart."

I am not saying that God caused my son's retardation to answer my prayer. The implications of that concept are far too complex for my simple understanding. I am saying He used the situation as a force to shape my life and help me become what I have become in Him. Thirty-two years later, I can truthfully say I wouldn't trade Treg for a son who is an All-American quarterback. He is truly a gift from God and an amazing young man. I often refer to him as our Holy Spirit hound dog. He has an amazing sensitivity to the Spirit of God and in his own simple and nonthreatening way has touched countless people with the simplicity of his relationship with and openness to God.

Standing Alone

The second defining moment of my life came during a season of ministry in which I learned the necessity of being able to stand alone. This was a time in my life when I learned the difference between faith and trust. I learned that faith relates to the power of God and trust relates to the character of God. I learned that it's one thing to have faith and another to trust God still when he says no or when things don't turn out the way we expected.

During this time I was one of several pastors in our church and enjoyed a wonderful experience teaching, writing, and traveling. I would occasionally be gone from our church for short periods of time, and when I came back I would become aware of something I hadn't seen before. I began to see that we weren't doing what we thought we were doing and had in fact entered a season of spiritual stagnation. I lacked the maturity to know how to share what I saw with others, and my attempts to do so were soon interpreted in a completely different way than I intended.

In short, I found myself standing alone.

In a meeting of the pastors and leaders of the congregation, I was removed as one of the pastors of the church. A few minutes after I walked into the meeting, I walked out in shock. I was unemployed, confused, and overwhelmed with fear. I was not given the kind of severance package that normally accompanies this type of thing. My income was cut severely and was only available for a few weeks. I was told to move out of my office immediately and that I would not be given an opportunity to say good-bye to the congregation. Worst of all, the congregation was never told that I had been removed. The implication was that I had quit because I was determined to start another church and that the leadership had tried to reason with me but I wouldn't listen.

I don't know how to describe the feelings of betrayal and personal doubt I experienced at this time. I've never felt as alone as I did then, but it was through this experience that God taught me one of the most important lessons I have ever learned.

During this time I went through a whole series of emotions. I went from shock and fear to moments of extreme anger and a desire to be sure everyone understood what had really happened. I felt the need to defend myself and fight back, but that wasn't what God let me do.

One day when I was splitting firewood, I began talking to the Lord about the possibility of splitting a few heads, and he spoke to me in a very simple and direct way. "Don't say a word," He said. "Don't defend yourself." I had to learn to trust Him to defend me and trust Him for the results, rather than taking care of it myself as I wanted to. I never was given an opportunity to explain my side of the situation, but during that time I learned one of the most valuable lessons of life.

One day after the anger subsided and my emotions had returned to normal, I asked God why this had happened. I wasn't challenging Him; I just wanted to know what he wanted to teach me through the whole experience. His answer was short and direct. "I wanted you to feel what that was like so you would never do it to someone else." I realized how important it is for those in leadership to be confident and secure in their own identity so they don't become a hindrance in the development and growth of others. The grace-based life does not focus on limiting others; it focuses on helping others realize the full possibilities of their lives. It helps others become all they can be. But people who are in a position to serve others in this way must be secure enough in their own identity and role to let that happen. This security most often develops through the moments and seasons of life when we learn to stand alone.

One day I was visiting with a man with a nation-wide ministry who was speaking in my new church. At one point in our conversation, he turned to me and said, "I visit many churches, but I hardly ever find the environment of freedom and participation that I sense here. People seem to be willing to serve and minister to others. It feels like a body and not just a one-man show."

That was a payoff moment for me. I had decided early in my ministry as a pastor that my job was to train and mobilize the people in the church to do the very things that many of them considered to be my job as the pastor. Here was someone from the outside confirming that at least to some degree my goal had become a reality, and it made me more than a little appreciative of what had happened in our congregation. Later as I was reflecting on this conversation, the Lord reminded me that without the moments of learning to stand alone that had occurred earlier in my life, I never would have developed the sense of personal security required to let others enjoy the freedom to try their own wings—and sometimes in the process to fly farther than I was ever able to fly. The grace-based life is the product of learning to stand alone.

Growing in Trust

The third defining moment for me in my pursuit of the grace-based life involved the importance of continuing to grow in my trust of God.

I had developed a slight sinus congestion and had gone to our family physician for some medication. As we were talking, I mentioned a small pain that I had been experiencing in my side, and the doctor began to ask me a few questions about it. I told him I thought I had strained a muscle in my rib area, but after a few questions, he said he thought it might be something else and wanted me to take a heart stress test, which I did a few days later.

After the test I went home to enjoy the Christmas season with my family, not even considering that there could be anything seriously wrong with my heart. About eleven that night, after we were all snug in our beds, the phone rang. It was the cardiologist who had performed the stress test earlier in the day. I wasn't quite ready for what he had to say.

"I know tomorrow is Christmas Eve," he began, "and I have been wrestling with whether to call you now or wait until after Christmas, but I decided it couldn't wait. I have scheduled an angiogram for you tomorrow morning at six at the hospital, and if it turns out the way I think it will, you need to be prepared to stay at the hospital."

The reality of what was going on still hadn't penetrated my sleepy mind, and I said, "Stay for what?"

"For open heart surgery. I think there is some serious blockage in your heart."

After giving a few more instructions on what to expect the next day, he hung up, and I went back to bed. I had to get up at four in order to be at the hospital on time.

Since all of this took place at the night, my wife and I had no opportunity to plan for someone to stay with the boys, so I told her I would drive myself to the hospital. My sons knew nothing of what had taken place during the night, and I didn't want to wake them so early, so I just quietly slipped into each of their rooms to check on them before I left for the hospital.

As I stood by their beds and watched them sleeping, my mind filled with special memories of each of them as smaller children and the reality that if something went wrong during the surgery, I might not be coming home and might not see them again. Perhaps that was the loneliest moment of my entire life. The idea that this was part of building a grace-based life never entered my mind, but I know today that it was.

I went on to the hospital, and on Christmas Eve had five-bypass open heart surgery, which turned out perfectly and literally saved my life.

About six months later, I was fully recovered from the surgery and life was pretty well back to normal when I got another call from our family physician. He said, "I wanted to wait until you got back on your feet before I called you, but you need to know that one of the blood tests we did during your surgery didn't come back the way it should. We need to schedule you for a biopsy to be sure you don't have prostate cancer." As it turned out, there was no cancer.

Until the heart surgery and cancer scare, like many people I had never really faced my own mortality; we are so busy living we never seriously think about dying. I am not suggesting that should become our focus, but during this time I learned something about what it means to live a grace-based life.

Death does not frighten me because I totally trust my future to God, but I've learned that while it is one thing to trust God for our own future, it might be a bigger challenge to trust Him for the future of our families when we think we might be gone. I found that the trust factor in my relationship with God had to be taken to a new level. I would like to tell you that this transition is complete, but I can't. I am still working on this one, which shows me that the process of building a grace-based life is a lifelong process. Therein lies its greatest challenge to our generation.

WHERE DOES GOD WANT TO TOTALLY IMMERSE YOU IN YOUR RELATIONSHIP WITH HIM?

We are a generation that holds out for the quick fix, the instant result, the best deal at the lowest possible price, but the grace-based life doesn't come quickly or cheaply. It comes at a cost; it will cost your life. If you are serious about living the grace-based life, you must understand how that takes place and embrace it.

You can firmly place this foundation stone in your relationship with God by asking several simple questions:

- What area of my relationship with Him needs to be totally immersed?
- What is He trying to establish as a foundational truth in my life?
- Is it in my willingness to be changed?
- Is it in some area where I struggle with sin?

- Is it in yielding to His will in some area of life?
- Is it in learning to know His power in my life?

God releases His grace in each of these areas when we let Him baptize us—totally immerse us in whatever aspect of our relationship with Him that He wants to establish in us. Chances are you face a situation or set of circumstances right now that He wants to use to turn some theory into firsthand experience for you. He wants to give you an unshakeable foundation strong enough to withstand the storms of life and support what He wants to build on it. But before He can do that, He must baptize you—totally immerse you in whatever you need to make your foundation complete.

The foundation stone of instruction about baptisms simply means being immersed in specific key areas of our relationship with God so they are no longer theory to us but something we know through firsthand experience. They become the spiritual foundation of our life and our relationship with Him.

In this chapter we have looked at how God allows things to happen *to* us that build something *in* us that He wants to release *through* us to fulfill His purpose *for* us. In the next chapter we will look at the question, Is the life I am living what God means when He talks about life?

CHAPTER 6

THE GRACE TO LIVE UNDER THE LAW OF BLESSING

YOU NEVER KNOW where or when or even how God is going to show you something that will increase your understanding of His ways or of the hunger of the human heart. One of those times for me took place when I was least expecting it and in a way that caught me off guard.

It was six in the morning. We were in the eighteenth hour of a twenty-four-hour prayer meeting when someone suggested I lay hands on those who would like to receive a pastoral blessing. I halfheartedly and sleepily agreed to invite anyone who wished to participate to come forward. I wasn't ready for what happened next.

Perhaps because I was getting tired and was ready to go home or maybe because I didn't really understand the power of blessing, I didn't expect much of a response. I thought a few struggling souls might venture forward in hope of some touch of encouragement, but to my surprise every single person in the auditorium lined up and waited for me to lay hands on them. I am sure for some it was only a religious exercise, but for the majority it turned out to be much more.

I wasn't sure what to do or even say, so I kept it simple. I merely placed one hand gently on the shoulder and head of each person in line and said, "I bless you with a pastor's blessing." As I did, some of those in line embraced me with such strength I could hardly move. Others wiped tears from their eyes, and others openly sobbed as they moved away from me. Some took a deep breath as if they were inhaling some tangible spiritual substance, while others sighed in an expression of soul-deep peace.

I had always believed in the idea of blessing, but what I experienced at that moment was more than an idea. I saw firsthand the power of blessing and the unmistakable evidence that we are created with not only a desire but with a heart-level need to be blessed. Furthermore, that experience helped me understand why the laying on of hands is a foundation stone for our lives.

AN EXPRESSION OF BLESSING

At first thought, laying on of hands doesn't seem to carry the same weight as the other five foundation stones referred to in Hebrew 6:1–3. I tended to think of it more as a ministry practice or technique than a foundational truth, because usually we find the practice of laying on of hands associated with other acts of ministry, such as praying for healing, impartation of spiritual gifts, baptism of the Holy Spirit, commissioning for ministry, or setting aside as spiritual leaders.

While all of these ministry practices are valid and important, it may be difficult to understand what they have to do with our personal relationship with God or our life experience unless we understand what they have in common. The common thread that holds all these ministry practices together is one simple dynamic: they are all expressions of blessing, of someone being blessed. Throughout Scripture we find an association between our hands and the concept of blessing. We lay hands on people to bless them in some expression of ministry to them and we "lift up holy hands" to bless God in worship. (I Tim 2:8)

But how is this foundational? What specific measure of grace is released through laying on of hands that enables us to build our lives on a foundation of grace?

LIVING UNDER THE LAW OF BLESSING

I think the answer is simple. The grace being released through laying on of hands allows our life to function under the law of blessing rather than the law of cursing. Specifically, it's the grace to live a blessed life as opposed to a cursed life, a life of possibilities rather than limitations.

Most people living in our culture and generation do not have a biblical understanding of the power of blessing or the power of cursing. We don't understand how either works or what it produces in an individual's life.

In biblical times, receiving a blessing—whether from a father, a king, or some other significant person—was so highly valued that people would resort to any measure to be the one blessed. We see this demonstrated in a passage describing Isaac and his twin sons, Jacob and Esau. Esau had been born first, and as such, was the one who would receive the patriarchal blessing as part of his birthright. Jacob was the younger twin, and because he understood the significance of the birthright blessing, he wanted it for himself. Their mother, Rebecca, also understood its significance. Because Jacob was her favorite, she wanted him to be the one who received the blessing, so she devised a plan that would deceive Isaac into giving it to Jacob.

The plan worked. When Isaac realized he had mistakenly given his blessing to the wrong son, he nearly had a stroke. When Esau realized his blessing had been stolen from him, he was devastated and begged his father to somehow bless him as well. When we read this dramatic account, it makes us wonder why Esau's loss of the blessing brought about such an extreme reaction. What did Isaac's family understand about blessing that we should understand?

In biblical culture a blessing contained legal power. It served much like a contract or a will does in our culture, and as such, it guaranteed certain privileges and provisions for the one who received it. In this instance, it guaranteed the largest portion of inheritance to the son who received the blessing. We can never fully understand this, however, until we understand that a blessing derives its power from the fact that it is, in effect, a spiritual law. A law is a principle to which there are no exceptions. Every time a law is applied, it produces the same result, without exception. If there were ever one exception, it would no longer be a law.

So when Genesis 27:33 says, "And indeed he will be blessed!" that is exactly what it means. Something will happen that can't be reversed or stopped. The blessing, with all its implications, will be established over Jacob's life.

Here's what we should understand. When we bless someone, either by laying hands on the person or by creating an environment of blessing in which the relationship can be nurtured to grow, we are in effect activating a spiritual law that will greatly influence what's going to happen in the person's life from that point on. And because blessing is a law, it guarantees the person will be established in certain key areas of life, specifically areas that relate to promise and potential. In other words, we are determining to a large degree whether the person's life will be lived under the law of blessing or the law of cursing.

What's the difference?

Probably the best way to answer this question is to identify some of the characteristics of a blessed life by looking at what the law of blessing produces when it is activated in someone's life. We can most easily do this by looking at what Isaac imparted to his son when he laid hands on him and blessed him.

A Blessed Life Has an Established Sense of Identity

The first thing Jacob received through his father's blessing was a sense of identity. When the law of blessing influences people, their lives will have a strong sense of identity; they will know who they are.

The first step in a deathbed blessing, which is what took place in the story of Isaac and his sons, was to ensure the identity of the one being blessed. The father would ask, "Are you my son?" and the son would respond accordingly. Jacob had to disguise himself and lie to Isaac and deceive him so he would unknowingly give his blessing to the wrong son.

There is tremendous power, strength, and stability released into our lives when we know who we are, when we have an established sense of identity. It keeps us from living with a counterfeit identity and a life of restless searching to know who we are.

I was having lunch with a pastor friend one day who had asked me if I was interested in serving on the leadership board of a local Christian organization. After we discussed all that was involved in doing so, I politely thanked him for considering me but said I really wasn't interested in his offer. The organization was an excellent group, and they were providing a much needed and admirable service to the body of Christ at large, but I knew I would not enjoy it and thus would not do a good job for them.

When I explained my feelings to my friend, he surprised me by saying, "Tom, I envy you."

I asked him why and he explained, "It's simple. You know who you are. You're not restless, searching for some new place to minister. You're content and comfortable with yourself."

To me, that was evidence that the law of blessing was at work in my life, for which I am extremely grateful to God.

My wife and I have three adopted sons, and we knew they, like many who are adopted, could face some identity issues in their lives, so we have worked hard to help them establish their identities and be at peace with who they are. We've helped them discover areas of interest that are unique to each of them and have encouraged them to develop those areas fully as a way of further establishing their identity.

We live in a generation in which many people either do not know who they are or are not at peace with who they are, and it causes all types of conflict and trouble. Probably nowhere is it more evident than in the so-called battle of the sexes or the confusion often associated with sexual identity, as demonstrated in the growth of the gay and lesbian movement. We see an increasing number of men trying to establish their identity by taking on characteristics and roles associated with the female sex and women doing the same thing by taking on characteristics and roles associated with the male sex. Any time a person tries to find fulfillment in life by taking on the characteristics of opposite sex, the unfortunate result is that he or she will move into confusion and further frustration.

These are signs of people who don't know who they are, who don't have an established sense of identity. Furthermore, it is indicative of a life with a weak foundation, unable to survive the storms of life or support what God wants to build on it.

A Blessed Life Has an Established Sense of Security and Well-Being

When I grew up, I always thought my family was rich. We certainly didn't qualify as rich, even though we never went without anything we needed. In fact, money was never an issue or a focus in our family. We didn't talk about it nor were we overly concerned about. While money was part life, it was never the reason for life. Yet somehow I always felt rich. I've come to understand that I felt that way because my parents had created a home environment where we always felt secure, with a sense that everything would be OK—there would be enough.

That was the second thing Jacob received through his father's blessing, another characteristic of a life lived under the law of blessing: a sense of security and well-being. When we live under the law of blessing, we live with confident, positive expectations. We don't live in fear of tomorrow, nor do we live in fear of something going wrong. We will always feel secure enough to give to others, because we don't live in fear of not having enough for themselves. The law of blessing creates an inner freedom that allows us to be generous.

Some lives are shaped by two constant fears, the fear of something going wrong and the fear of never having enough. Both are signs of the law of cursing at work. When we are concerned that something will go wrong or that tomorrow we might lose everything we own, we will never feel free to become givers. Our concern for protecting and keeping what we have prevents us from thinking of others.

Generosity, then, is a sign of a blessed life.

A Blessed Life Has an Established Sense of Destiny

Another sign of a blessed life is an established sense of destiny. All blessings contain the seed of promise and potential; they point the individual to the destiny God has established for them.

As a husband, father, and pastor, I want to create an environment in my marriage, home, and church where the seeds of potential can grow and produce a great harvest in the lives of the people in my life. I firmly believe that one of the primary tests of godly leadership is the degree to which those under that leadership realize and develop their God-ordained destiny.

Take marriage as an example. The proof of a good and godly husband is the degree to which his wife blossoms and becomes the woman God created her to be, not the degree to which the marriage operates in order. As important as biblical order is in marriage, it's not the primary proof that the marriage operates under the law of blessing. When a woman has a man in her life who relates to her on the basis of the law of blessing, she doesn't find it necessary to become part of some worldly organization or movement in order to find her identity. She finds her identity in a mutually beneficial way within their relationship through her own freedom and her husband's encouragement.

I am convinced that every life contains the seeds of potential and promise. Every human heart contains a sense of destiny, a hope and dream for fulfillment and significance, a desire to know that we matter and that our life has made a difference. In an environment of blessing, those seeds of promise can grow and produce. That's what the law of blessing does. It reaches into the human heart and nurtures that seed of identity. It waters and nourishes it with grace from the heart of the Creator who put it there in the first place. It turns potential into destiny realized.

In the forty years I have served as a pastor in the body of Christ, I have been amazed time after time at the power of the law of blessing. When an environment of blessing became prevalent in the life of a congregation, I have seen people of doubtful potential become giants in the kingdom of God. People who seemed to possess little promise have become oaks of righteousness and sources of strength to others.

If I could, I would lay hands on every person who reads this book and ask God to release the law of blessing on your life. I would ask God to give you a sense of identity as a child of God, a sense of security and well-being for every aspect of life, and an established sense of destiny that calls into existence the seed of promise God placed in your heart when He created you.

I would ask God to move you out from under the law of cursing—a spiritual law that places limits on your potential and promise—and place you under the influence of the law of blessing so you can experience the benefits of divine favor released into your lives. I would pray that you would walk with the favor of God in everything you do, that you would hear the Father's words whispered into your souls, "This is my child, in whom I am well pleased," and live with the confident expectancy produced by those words.

That's what I would do if I could, but even though I can't lay hands on my readers and release the law of blessing on all of you, there is no reason it can't happen anyway. God will release the law of blessing on every person who relates to Him in faith and obedience to His word.

So from the perspective of the law of blessing, we see how the laying on of hands is foundational.

Laying on of hands releases the grace to live a blessed life, to live with the favor of God permeating and strengthening every aspect of life and assuring that your life will fulfill the destiny God had in mind for it at the moment it was created.

Now let's turn to the next stone in our foundation—the grace to live a resurrected life—and discover how eternal life affects every area of our life.

CHAPTER 7

THE GRACE TO LIVE
A RESURRECTED LIFE

WHEN MANY PEOPLE hear the term *the resurrection of the dead*, they tend to think primarily in terms of something that will take place in the future, but that can be a mistake. While the resurrection of the dead certainly does have a future application, it is also a part of our present-day relationship with God. In fact, it is a major part of the grace-based life because the grace released to us when this foundation stone is firmly in place in our life is what enables us to live a normal Christian life.

If you have ever started a project only to discover partway through the process that you needed help to finish what you started, then you will understand why this specific measure of grace is so important. At some point after we have become Christians, most of us discover we are going to need some serious help to see this new life through to a successful conclusion. This is why the resurrection of the dead is a foundational issue in our spiritual development.

To some degree all of us begin our relationship with God in the same condition Lazarus was in when Jesus transformed his life. When Jesus stood outside Lazarus's grave and called him back to life, Lazarus did indeed receive new life, but when he exited his grave he did so still bound by graveclothes. As a result he couldn't walk normally nor could he see clearly. In other words, he was unable to express life the way God meant it to be expressed. Not only did he need Jesus to bring him back to life, he also needed Jesus to free him from the restraints that were still on him because of his previous condition.

Many of God's people are like that. Even though we receive new life, our ability to express our new life is limited. We haven't yet discovered how to walk in the ways of God, nor can we see with eyes of faith and hope because we are still bound by the garments of death associated with our former life.

That's why the resurrection of the dead is foundational. The resurrection of the dead is the process by which God removes the graveclothes that bind us and frees us to live a normal Christian life.

How does this process work?

Two Spiritual Laws That Affect Everything

In Romans 8:2 we are introduced to a pair of spiritual laws that have the potential to affect our life in significant ways: the law of sin and death and the law of the Spirit of life in Christ Jesus. Without exception, every life and every area of every life is subject to one of these two spiritual laws.

We need to know, of course, what this means and how it affects our spiritual walk and development. What does it mean to be under the law of sin and death? What does it mean to be under the law of Spirit of life in Christ Jesus?

Basically, being under the law of sin and death means that every life and every part of life that is subject to the law of sin and death is going to die—no exceptions. Sin brings the touch of death to anything and everything that comes under its influence and power. To say it another way, sin eventually kills everything it controls.

The Wages of Sin Is Separation

Romans 6:23 tell us, "The wages of sin is death." Wages are what we get paid for our service or labor; if we serve sin, it will pay us with death. To understand how this relates in practical terms to everyday life, let's paraphrase the verse this way: "The wages of sin is not just death; the wages of sin is also separation." Death always brings some kind of separation. In other words, living under the power of the law of sin and death means I will experience some significant separations in my life.

For example, spiritual death as wages of sin means the law of sin and death separates people from God. According to the Bible, anyone who does not have a faith relationship with Jesus Christ is separated from God. Jesus Christ bridges the gap that separates sinful man from God and makes it possible for us to be in contact with God.

Relational death as wages of sin separates people from people. Since we live all of life in relationship to someone or something, conflicts in relationships can bring death to those relationships, whether with another person or in some area of life. We live our marriage and family life in relationship to our spouse and children and our work life in relationship with co-workers and others with whom we have contact through our occupation or profession.

The same thing holds true with every area or aspect of life, including our finances, health, and leisure time. We live within the sphere of relationships, and each area of life is subject to the law of sin and death, which means each of these relationships will experience some degree of conflict and fall short of its potential because of the law of sin and death.

Marriages experience conflict. Families experience conflict. Personal finances experience conflict. Social relationships and work relationships experience conflict all for the same reason. The influence of the law of sin and death in some way affects these relationships. "The wages of sin is death," or some type of separation.

The same thing is true in the physical realm. Physical death as wages of sin separates our soul from our body. We all understand that at some point everyone dies. Everyone's soul is separated from the body, which happens because of the power of the law of sin and death over creation.

Death was not part of God's original plan for creation. Death was introduced into creation through sin, and the law of sin and death eventually became one of the controlling factors of creation. Every life, every area of life, and every relationship in life is subject to the law of sin and death's influence and power until we receive the grace from God we need to set us free from its influence, which the resurrection of the dead is able to do. But until that happens, we will continue to live under the law of sin and death and will continue to experience significant separations in all areas of life.

Reversing the Law of Sin and Death

However, Romans 6:23 not only says that the wages of sin is death; it also goes on to say that "the gift of God is eternal life in Christ Jesus our Lord."

Probably all of us at some time in our lives have made the mistake of thinking of eternal life as human life that goes on forever and ever, but that is not eternal life. It certainly includes the forever aspect, but it is much more than that.

In reality there are four types of life in creation, four distinct life forms: plant life, animal life, human life, and eternal life. We need to understand eternal life as a specific life form, as separate and distinct from other life forms as animal life is from plant life and human life. Eternal life is not an extension of human life; it is a new form of life.

What does the Bible say happens when a person is "born again"? (John 3:16) In 2 Corinthians 5:17 we read, "If anyone is in Christ, he is a new creation." In other words, he is a new life form.

Making you born again is not God's way of polishing up your old life or cleaning up the old you. It is God's way of re-creating you. It is God's way of letting you start over as a new person. You are born again as a new creation, and God replaces the old human life with the new eternal life. But that is not all that happens. This new life form that you have become, this new creation in Christ, is an expression or extension of the resurrection life of Christ, and as such, it is not subject to the control or influence of the law of sin and death.

This new creation that you have become operates under a different spiritual law, the law of the Spirit of life in Christ Jesus.

Here is the really good news. The law of the Spirit of life in Christ Jesus covers everything previously covered by the law of sin and death. It covers our spiritual life, our relational life, and our physical life. Every part of life comes under the influence and potential control of this new law, the law of the Spirit of life in Christ Jesus. The foundation stone of the resurrection of the dead simply means everything that died because of sin can now live because of Jesus Christ and His resurrection.

Because of the grace available through this foundation stone, I can have a resurrected relationship with God, I can have a resurrected marriage, I can have a resurrected family, and I can have resurrected finances, health, career, or business. The resurrection of the dead means that because of grace, everything that operated under the law of sin and death can be moved over to the law of the Spirit of life in Christ Jesus.

Furthermore, the resurrection of the dead promises us a future, assures us of tomorrow, and offers us hope. Everything once separated by death can be reunited in Christ. The wages of sin may be separation, but the gift of God is a new form of life that brings it all back together again.

Have you ever felt as if your life or some part of your life was falling apart? When that happens, the law of sin and death is at work, but because of the resurrection of Jesus Christ and the resurrection power available to all who are "in Christ," everything threatening to fall apart can be put back together again. Wholeness and completion form the basic nature of salvation and result from the grace available to us through the resurrection of the dead.

Wholeness and completion don't just happen in some sort of magical vacuum, however. They result directly from one of the most critical spiritual resources we have at our disposal: the creative work of the Holy Spirit.

THE CREATIVE WORK OF THE SPIRIT OF GOD

Genesis 1:1–25 gives us the biblical account of creation and tells us how the world, heavens, and life came into existence. This important passage of Scripture not only shows us that God is the source of creation and the author of life, it also introduces us to the creative work of the Spirit of God and God's strategy for providing what is missing in our lives and development as His people.

The pattern or formula you see here in the creation account is the way God still works in individual lives and situations. What the Spirit of God did in creation, He waits to do in your life and life situation. Many of us tend to resist or ignore the ministry and place of the Spirit of God in our lives and relationships, which is a major mistake because we shut ourselves off from His creative work and all that He provides for our development.

Just as in this passage in Genesis, the Spirit of God hovers over your life situation, over those things that seem to be falling apart, waiting for the Father to tell him what to create. When the Spirit of God hears the Father say, "Let there be . . ." He leaps into action and begins to create what the Father has spoken, which always exactly fits the need in each situation.

The creation account tells us that in the beginning "the earth was formless and empty, darkness was over the surface of the deep" (v. 2). Creation was not yet what God intended it to be, so He called on the creative work of the Spirit of God to bring about the finished product.

Creating What Is Lacking

The Spirit of God creates what isn't there, to begin the process of directing things to become what God intended them to be, to create what is missing, to bring things to completion. God had a vision of what creation would look like and how it would work. The Spirit of God's assignment was to carry out that design.

First, the Spirit of God brings order and fullness to a situation. Let's say you have a difficult relationship with someone. The truth is you don't like the person much, let alone love him or her, but you don't want it to be that way. You wish your heart were tender toward this person, that love would be there naturally. What do you do? How do you develop that love?

This kind of life situation is the type of challenge where we need the creative ministry of the Spirit of God. If you try to accomplish what you want through your own strength and efforts, you will end in frustration and failure. You will soon become exhausted and discouraged, and chances are you will give up with the self-condemning thought that you are a total failure and will never become the person you want to be. It is to people like this that Jesus said, "Come to me, all you who are weary and burdened, and I will give you rest" (Matt. 11:28).

8 7

If there is any secret to living the Christian life successfully, it is this: Don't try to do the Spirit of God's job; it will wear you out. Only the Spirit of God can create the change in your attitude and relationship with another person and turn it into what God intended. Only He can create the love that is missing.

There was a season in my life when I struggled with prayer. I didn't like to pray, nor did I have any desire to pray. I tried everything I (or anyone else) could think of to become a person of prayer. No matter how hard I tried, all my efforts produced failure and condemnation, because I needed a desire and a vision for prayer, and I was unable to produce those through my own strength.

Finally, I gave up and began to ask the Holy Spirit to create a desire to pray within me. Every time the thought came to me throughout the day, I would simply say, "Holy Sprit, give me the desire to pray." Some days I probably repeated that simple little prayer as many as fifty times. Then one day after for several months, I was sitting at my desk when much to my surprise and delight I became aware of a strong desire to spend time with God and pray. Prayer for me moved from a place of duty to a place of desire as the Spirit of God completely transformed my prayer life.

I know the change I experienced was the result of the creative work of the Spirit of God and not the result of my self-effort or strength. He was the one who turned my situation into what God intended.

The Spirit of God can create what's missing or incomplete in all of us and our life situations. Our place is to ask Him to begin his creative work in us.

Creating a Solid Place to Stand

But the creative work of the Spirit of God doesn't stop with our individual situations. When things are falling apart in our world, what do we really need? What do we look for in the midst of a major storm? I think we would all agree that in those moments, we search for something to take hold of, something solid that will give us an anchor in the storm.

According to Genesis 1:9, that's the second thing the Spirit of God creates for us. In the midst of a world of chaos and turmoil, He looks at our situation and says, "Let dry ground appear." He gives us a solid place to stand.

Faith produces a substantive reality inside us. According to Hebrews 11:1, "Now faith is being sure of what we hope for and certain of what we do not see." It is the result of God's Word applied to our need through the Spirit of God. Faith gives us a solid place to stand.

I have shared how real God's peace became to my wife, Jeanne, and me in light of the difficult experiences regarding our son's handicap. The Word of God, plus the creative work of the Holy Spirit, provided a solid place to stand in that season of chaos and uncertainty, a place to stand that's very, very real to us.

Romans 8:28 says, "And we know that in all things God works for the good of those who love him, who have been called according to his purpose." This is a powerful truth that gives us solid footing during times of chaos and uncertainty. I am absolutely convinced that every difficult season and experience of life—including the incidents I have mentioned—have been used by God to build something solid in my life. Even this conviction exists because the Holy Spirit created it. He alone changed my thinking from a human perspective that despises or seeks to avoid difficult experiences to a heavenly perspective that embraces the challenges of life as expressions of God's grace, as gifts God designed to help me become the person He created me to be.

Creating Resources for Everyday Living

Other parts of the Holy Spirit's act of creation in Genesis 1 illustrate how He provides what may be incomplete in our lives:

- Let the trees bear *fruit* (v. 11);
- Let there be *light* (v. 14);
- Let the land produce living creatures—*life* (v. 24).

I believe each of these represents what He is really trying to produce or create in us:

Fruit represents His desire to create the character of Christ in each of us: what the Bible calls the fruit of the Spirit.

Light represents the wisdom and understanding we need in order to live life as God designed it. The Bible tells us in Psalm 119:105 that His word is a lamp to our feet—giving us step-by-step directions as we follow Him on a daily basis—and a light to our path—providing the wisdom we need to set the direction of our life.

Life represents the new life we receive from Him as well as the strength we need to complete our journey.

Many times when things are not the way God intended them to be, we don't survive the times of chaos or the seasons of life, because these elements–fruit, light, and life—are missing from our lives. For example, have you ever faced a situation where you didn't even know how to pray with wisdom or understanding about the situation or need? That's what Paul refers to in 1 Corinthians 2:9–16, which tells us that no one can know what God has prepared for us unless the Holy Spirit reveals it to us. Paul refers to situations where we need revelation even to proceed in prayer and wisdom to know how to act.

That's what the Holy Spirit creates for us: direction in prayer and ability to pray with the mind of Christ. That's why praying in the Spirit is so important. It taps into the understanding God has about a situation and gets to the real issues. For years, my personal habit and practice has been to first pray in the Spirit until there is some understanding or direction and then begin to pray with understanding. Once I have God's perspective on the situation, I can articulate my desire and requests with a new level of confidence and faith.

When your child is going through a difficult season, for example, don't pray only for his or her deliverance from the challenge. Get God's perspective—find out what He is trying to work into the child's life through this situation and pray with confidence that it will be accomplished.

In times of chaos and challenge, we need strength to finish the journey. Often we give up or quit just before God has finished something He wants to do in our lives. Our greatest need at those moments is for the Holy Spirit to create the endurance we need for the second mile, because many times the results we are looking for are not produced until we are in the second mile. I've learned not to be impressed by how people begin their journey; I want to see how they finish. For example, as wonderful and delightful as they are, weddings don't impress me, but I am impressed with fifty-year anniversaries.

Many of our struggles are long lasting. Some last a lifetime, and when that is the case we need the kind of strength available to us through the creative work of the Holy Spirit. We all come to points where we need to be refreshed and restrengthened for the journey we are on, and because His mercies are new every morning (Lam. 3:23 KJV), we can be assured that through this major part of the Holy Spirit's creative ministry to us, we can continue on with His life flowing through us.

Let's bring this chapter to a close by asking the simple question, where do you need the creative work of the Holy Spirit in your life?

Do you need His creative work for something that's missing, something that is still incomplete and not yet what God intended it to be?

Do you simply need a solid place to stand?

Do you need wisdom, understanding, and new strength for your journey?

Remember this, the grace available to you as a child of God through the resurrection of the dead is what the Holy Spirit did in creation. He not only can but wants to do this creative work in your life.

CHAPTER 8

THE GRACE TO CHOOSE WISELY

PART OF ANY building project is deciding what types of materials to use to complete the project and ensure that we are building a strong and solid building. That's where the foundational stone of eternal judgment comes in. The foundational stone of eternal judgment gives us the grace to choose wisely. When this foundation stone is in place and producing what God intended it to produce in our lives, we will be able to choose our building materials with wisdom.

According to Scripture, we can choose to build with hay, wood, and straw, or we can choose to build with gold, silver, and precious stones. Our choice matters, because what we build will be tested. Scripture states, "His work will be shown for what it is, because the Day will bring it to light" (1 Cor. 3:13).

As I begin to build on the foundation, I need to make wise choices about what kinds of building materials I use, and that is where the grace associated with eternal judgment enters the picture.

Verse 10 in this same passage shows us the relationship between grace and the ability to build with wisdom. "By the grace God has given me, I laid a foundation as an expert builder, and someone else is building on it. But each one should be careful how he builds." Let me paraphrase this passage with a personal application: "You have put down a foundation and now you are ready to build on it. What you need next is wisdom to choose the types of building materials that will stand the tests you will face in the future."

I think we all understand that how a life turns out can often be traced to choices that were made at some stage in the development of that life. In this chapter we will look at some of the choices that would qualify to be called wise choices, but before we do that, let's look at the basic nature of the options we have.

Essentially, we choose between eternal values and temporal values as building materials of our lives. Choosing temporal values means we have chosen to focus our lives on things that impress people but are temporary in nature—things such as status, success, wealth, fame, and power. In 1 Corinthians 3:12 (NIV) the Bible refers to these values as hay, wood, and straw.

In the same passage we are told we can choose rather to build with gold, silver and costly stones, things that are permanent in nature, things which represent eternal values, and things that matter to God.

That's the basic question we answer in our choice of building materials: am I building my life focusing on things that impress people or things that matter to God, things that the world values or that God values? Am I building only for today, or am I building with eternity in mind?

Let's suppose you decide you want to build with gold, silver, and precious stones; with the things God sees as important. What things do you choose? Rather than trying to get specific in answering that question, let's look at several principles that can help us make wise choices as we build our lives.

PURSUE WISDOM

"Wisdom is supreme; therefore get wisdom. Though it cost all you have, get understanding" (Prov. 4:7). According to this verse, wisdom relates to understanding, but understanding what?

First, we need to understand that wisdom has nothing to do with intelligence, which is actually a temporal value. Intelligence is one of those things that impress people. I certainly don't mean to suggest that intelligence is a bad thing, but I have to say that some of the most intelligent people I have known showed the most ignorance when it came to understanding life and how to live it. To my way of thinking, understanding how life really works—what it takes to make it work, what is important and what is not—is the very essence of wisdom. Living life the way God designed it is what matters to God.

The Bible says, "The fear of the LORD is the beginning of wisdom" (Prov. 9:10), which tells me that I will never understand how God designed my life to be lived if I don't start with the spiritual dimension. But how often do we see the "experts" in our generation try to explain how we are to live while never addressing the spiritual dimension of life? For example, time after time we see this lack of wisdom demonstrated on news programs as reports on some human activity or failure are explained as financial, educational, or social issues while the spiritual dimension of life is never mentioned, despite being foundational to all of life's activities and conditions.

Choosing to build with gold, silver, and precious stones as building materials means we must pursue wisdom, because without it we will never understand how God designed life to work or what it takes to make it work.

When I was between eight and ten years old, my Sunday school class in the little church where I grew up learned about King Solomon, the man referred to in the Bible as a man with great understanding and wisdom (1 Kings 3:6-9 NKJV). I was so impressed by that story, and especially by God's response to Solomon when he asked God for wisdom, that I left class that day asking God for wisdom in my life. From that time on, understanding what it takes to make life work as God designed it became a major focus in my life and my relationship with God. Several things I've learned have been especially helpful to me in that pursuit. I believe they will help you, as well.

Reading Proverbs Everyday

The first has been my practice of reading from the book of Proverbs nearly every day, reading the chapter that corresponds with the day's date. I am simple enough to believe that this plan might be what God had in mind when He gave us this collection of His wisdom about life and how to live it. First and foremost, Proverbs is about wisdom, and God promises wisdom to those who read this book. It teaches us how life really works, what is important, and what is not.

Several years ago I was watching a news talk show, and the topic of the evening was the latest scandal by a national politician. The format of the program consisted of a panel of experts. Each was asked what he or she thought the politician should do to get out of the mess he had created. All but one panelist gave typical political-expert opinions. One panelist, however, had different answers, and as the program developed he began to dominate the discussion. Before long the others were listening to him with wonderment at the profound responses he gave.

As I listened, it suddenly dawned on me that he was paraphrasing Proverbs in many of his statements. He didn't say, "The Bible says . . ." but simply responded to the situation from a biblical perspective. I don't know if he was a believer, but he clearly demonstrated an understanding of the real issues in the situation. He came off as a very wise man, because his wisdom could be traced to biblical principles.

Proverbs will give you wisdom and an understanding of how life really works.

Interpreting the Natural by the Spiritual

Learning to interpret the natural side of life by the spiritual dimension of life has been very helpful to me as well. Paul gives us the principle of first the natural, then the spiritual in 1 Corinthians 15:46.

The natural side of life illuminates the spiritual side of life. In other words, what is happening or what I am witnessing on the surface of a situation is not the real issue or reality. I need to look behind the natural expression and discover the spiritual root, cause, and dynamic. Before I can really understand the natural, I have to see the spiritual dimension.

One expression of wisdom is the ability to see the connection between the natural and spiritual aspects of life, to see the spiritual reality demonstrated through the natural situation.

When the politician I mentioned earlier was going through the problems he faced because of his failure, one of the most common comments we heard at that time was, "Well, that's his personal life. It doesn't affect how he does his job." I found it frightening that a large number of people actually seemed to believe that there was no relationship between personal life and job performance. A majority of our generation clearly demonstrated that they didn't understand the principle of first the natural, then the spiritual.

What we see in the natural expression of a person's life demonstrates the true inner condition of that life. What we see on the outside reflects what is going on or not going on inside. Wisdom says to look at the natural to understand the spiritual, and you will understand how things really are.

Choosing Spiritual Leaders We Follow

I have found the principle of "first the natural, then the spiritual" extremely helpful in choosing the spiritual leaders I choose to follow and allow to influence my life;

Often believers choose their leaders on the basis of temporal values—things that will impress people—such as personality, charisma, decisiveness, experience, or maybe a strong business sense. People often also ask, do they prophesy? Have they memorized the Bible? Do they demonstrate certain specific spiritual gifts? While these qualifications can be very helpful, wisdom says to look at other qualifications also. Here are some of the questions I ask when I am looking for spiritual leaders, whether men or women:

How do they treat their spouses?

Do they wash their cars?

Do they pay their bills?

Do they mow their lawns?

Why do I ask such unspiritual-sounding questions? The reason is not only simple; it is also biblical. If we are unfaithful in these areas, we will be in other areas also. I know that people who treat these things carelessly will treat the things of God carelessly as well—including the lives of those they are called to serve.

That's the foundation of wisdom at work in a critical area of life, the first step to building with gold, silver, and precious stones as we choose the leaders who will impact and influence our lives.

EMBRACE AUTHORITY

Remember our goal to choose wisely as we select the building materials we will use to construct our life. Embracing the principle of submission to authority is one of the wisest choices anyone can make.

This is true for two key reasons. First, to resist authority means to resist God himself. "He who rebels against authority is rebelling against what God has instituted, and those who do so will bring judgment on themselves" (Rom. 13:2). When we resist or reject the principle of embracing authority, we align ourselves with the kingdom of darkness. It means we have embraced the spirit in which Satan operates, and that can never be a wise way to build our lives.

God planned authority to provide protection and blessing to us. I am certainly not so naive as to suggest that people in authority always act the way they should or always do what we want them to do, but I am suggesting that to rebel against the authorities God has placed in our lives only adds to the problem.

When we are faced with bad authority, we should understand three things about embracing the principle of authority as we build our lives.

First, we can disobey bad authority and still maintain a submissive spirit. The attitude and spirit in which we respond is the ultimate issue. In other words, we can disobey in submission and obey in rebellion. Anyone who has ever raised and disciplined a two-year-old understands this concept. A child told to sit down may be sitting down on the outside while standing up on the inside.

Second, if we maintain a submissive attitude, God will eventually work in the situation and change the offending authority. Often we are tempted to use the failure of those in authority in our life as an excuse to reject the whole concept of submission to authority, but that is a mistake. When that happens, not only does God have to deal with the bad authority, but He also has to deal with the condition of our heart, which simply makes the entire process that much longer and more complicated.

To relate to authority requires us to walk in faith. Matthew 8:5–11 tells us of a Roman centurion who had a servant who needed healing. When he approached Jesus with his request, Jesus implied He would come to the man's house to meet with the servant, to which the centurion responded, "I too am a man under authority, and I know that all you have to do is speak the word and my servant will be healed" (v. 9, author's paraphrase).

When Jesus heard the man's response, He replied that this was the greatest expression of faith He had witnessed in the entire country. Yet the centurion had said nothing about his own level of faith; he spoke only of his understanding of the principle of being under authority. Submission to authority means we have chosen to take the situation out of our hands and place it in the hands of God, which is always a wise decision.

Building your life around the principle of authority is one of the wisest choices you can make. It will build your faith as well as provide God's blessing and protection.

There is, however, one more extremely important principle we need to consider as we choose the building materials we will use in building the foundation of our life.

VALUE THOSE AREAS OF LIFE THAT GOD HAS SET ASIDE

There are certain areas of life God has set aside for His own unique purposes. Because they have been set aside to the purposes of God, these areas are considered holy, and we are warned not to profane them by treating them as if they hold no special value to God.

To profane something basically means to make it common by removing the distinctiveness God placed on it. To do so is never a wise choice, especially when it comes to choosing the materials by which we will build our lives.

Let me give you several key areas of life where the attitude and practice of our generation and culture have taken areas of life set aside for the unique purposes of God and profaned them, treated them with disrespect.

Marriage

Perhaps nothing illustrates this point more than the evolving attitude in our generation undermining traditional marriage. The unique design and pattern for marriage found in Scripture, one man and one woman in a covenant relationship, is being challenged by other practices and attitudes, such as living together as husband and wife without being officially married and living together in same-sex unions. In either case, something set apart by God for His unique purpose is being reduced to something far less than God had in mind. That which is holy becomes profane.

Sabbath

The same thing has happened to the practice of honoring the Sabbath. In our culture the practice of setting aside one day of the week in recognition and honor of the Lord has been lost. Sundays, for example, are treated like any other day of the week. Not only is it business as usual, but this day designed for worship and honoring the Lord has become instead a day dedicated to idolatry. Sports, business, and other leisure activities are pitted against worship services, and a day set aside for God has been profaned—made common, like every other day of the week.

Tithe

How do you profane the tithe? When you don't tithe, you will end up using that which should be set aside for God's purposes for your own purposes. When we treat the tithe like the rest of our finances, we make it common and rob it of its holy nature. It becomes profane.

The bottom line is that profaning the holiness attached to any area of life is an attack against God himself, who is holy. That is not a wise way to go about building your life.

Pursuing wisdom, embracing authority, and valuing what is holy will give you a foundation of grace for making wise choices in life. If you make specific choices within the context of these kingdom principles, you will build with gold, silver, and precious stones, and what you build will stand in the face of eternal judgment.

EPILOGUE: THE GRACE TO FINISH WITH NO REGRETS

OVER THE YEARS I have noticed that most people come to the end of their journey in one of two ways. Some finish like Abraham, who "died happy at a ripe old age, full of years" (Gen. 25:8 MSG) while others come to the end of their time filled with thoughts of what might have been. The difference is found in one very simple and basic truth: a grace-based life finishes with no regrets. Those who learn to live in the freedom and power of grace will finish in the freedom and power of grace.

The question you must answer is, How do you want to finish? Do you want to try to finish in the strength of self-effort, or would you rather finish in the power and freedom of letting God do for you those things in life you are unable to do for yourself?

If you opt for the second choice, you will need to look at how Jesus transformed a single loaf of bread into enough bread to feed several thousand people, because what He did to the bread is what He will need to do to your life. When this process of transformation begins to happen, we are well on our way to building a grace-based life and finishing with no regrets.

Jesus started by taking the bread. The first step to the grace-based life is to allow the Lord to take control of our lives, which means coming to a place of surrender. "Not my will, but yours be done" (Luke 22:42) are the words that open the door to the grace-based life.

He then blessed the bread. The act of surrendering our will to the Lord moves us into a new spiritual environment in which the law of blessing begins to work in our lives. Circumstances and situations begin to change, and the things that seemed to work against us now begin to work for us. We begin experiencing the favor of God in new ways.

He broke the bread. At this point in the transformational process, Jesus introduces us to the cross and invites us to die so that new life can be released through us. We learn that we don't have the personal resources to live the life to which we have been called. We relinquish self-effort and reliance on personal discipline and strength so He can do those things for us that we are unable to do for ourselves.

He gave the bread away. Many believers have never understood that one of the reasons Jesus saves us is so He can give us away as salt and light to the generation in which we live. "Sir, . . .we would like to see Jesus" (John 12:21) is the heart cry of our generation. Not many are impressed with religion and religious organizations, but almost everyone will respond to a transformed life that reflects the character and Spirit of Jesus Christ. This transformation is a key to penetrating the shell of cynicism that surrounds our generation and culture, for the authenticity of a grace-based life is difficult to ignore or reject.

May the grace of God be with you as you seek to live a grace-based life.

LaVergne, TN USA
23 July 2010
190532LV00001BA/3/P

9 781414 113135